WITHDRAWN

Love

Julie Murray

abdopublishing.com

Published by Abdo Kids, a division of ABDO, PO Box 398166, Minneapolis, Minnesota 55439.
Copyright © 2017 by Abdo Consulting Group, Inc. International copyrights reserved in all countries.
No part of this book may be reproduced in any form without written permission from the publisher.

Printed in the United States of America, North Mankato, Minnesota.

052016

092016

Photo Credits: iStock, Shutterstock

Production Contributors: Teddy Borth, Jennie Forsberg, Grace Hansen

Design Contributors: Candice Keimig, Dorothy Toth

Cataloging-in-Publication Data

Names: Murray, Julie, author.

Title: Love / by Julie Murray.

Description: Minneapolis, MN : Abdo Kids, [2017] | Series: Emotions | Includes
    bibliographical references and index.

Identifiers: LCCN 2015959118 | ISBN 9781680805246 (lib. bdg.) |
    ISBN 9781680805802 (ebook) | ISBN 9781680806366 (Read-to-me ebook)

Subjects: LCSH: Love--Juvenile literature. | Emotions--Juvenile literature.

Classification: DDC 152.4--dc23

LC record available at http://lccn.loc.gov/2015959118

Table of Contents

Love

Love makes us feel **warm** inside.

It is an **emotion**.

Sue is a big sister.

She feels love.

We feel love from our family.

Mary cooks with her dad.

We feel love from our friends.

Danny plays with Josh.

We feel love from our pets.

Sam plays with his cat.

Bobby hugs his mom.

He feels love.

We can love doing things.

Kenny loves playing the piano.

Ellen loves baking.

She makes cookies.

When do you feel love?

Things to Do to Make Others Feel Loved

donate old clothes and toys

tell your friends when
they've done a good job

give someone a hug

write a letter to a loved one

Glossary

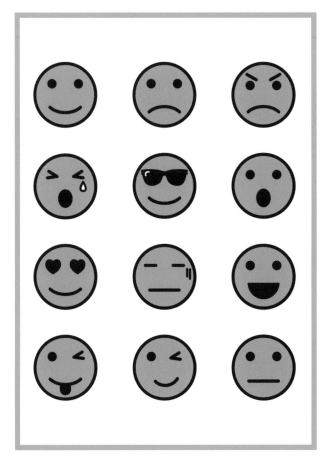

emotion
a strong feeling.

warm
a feeling of affection.

Index

abdokids.com

Use this code to log on to abdokids.com and access crafts, games, videos, and more!

Abdo Kids Code:
ELK5246